MARCH TO MARCH

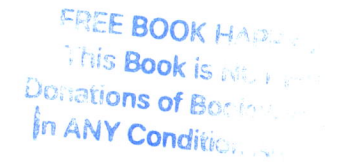

JOHN WILLIAMS

A BBTS Publication
Deri, Bargoed.
BBTS (Baarbaara The Sheep Publications)
Est. Feb 2012
email: **baarbaarathesheep@hotmail.co.uk**
baarbaarathesheep/wordpress.com

Baarbaara
The Sheep

© John Williams February 2023

ISBN: 9798376036716
Imprint: Independently published

KDP Assigned ISBN registered with Booksinprint.com

All rights reserved. No part of this publication may be reproduced, stored in a retrieval system or transmitted at any time by any means: electronic, mechanical, photocopying, recording or otherwise, without the prior permission of the copyright holders.

Typeset: Arial
All Poetry, Images & Layout by John Williams

To Mel's father, David Griffiths, who sadly passed away on December 18th 2022.

BIOGRAPHY

THIS IS JOHN'S 8TH BOOK. HE HAS ALSO WRITTEN FOR MANY OTHER PUBLICATIONS. JOHN WAS BORN AND GREW UP IN MERTHYR TYDFIL AND LIVES WITH PARTNER MEL GRIFFITHS IN LONDON. JOHN HAS PERFORMED AT NUMEROUS FESTIVALS SUCH AS MERTHYR RISING, LONDON'S ANARCHIST BOOK FAIR AND PUNK FESTIVALS AROUND THE COUNTRY. HE IS A MEMBER OF THE RED POETS AND ATTENDS PROTESTS WHEN ABLE, DUE TO DISABILITY.

OTHER BOOKS BY AUTHOR

SCREAM MACHINE
BLOOD CELLS
IN THE CITY
ANOTHER EMPTY CHAIR
KILLING TIME
SECRETS OF SUNLIGHT
FROST BITE

Introduction

March To March covers a journey over one year of the diagnosis of Cancers during the backdrop of the Covid landscape. Many illnesses were dismissed as long Covid. Followed by shock and the journey through HELL on earth that follows. I am forever grateful to the medical profession that saved my partner's life.

CONTENTS

1. DENTIST
2. Mental Dental Health
4. A Stranger's Wake Up Call

6. RADIOTHERAPY
8. Mesh Mask For My Beautiful Angel
10. Swiss Extract
11. Radiation Mesh Mask

12. ROYAL FREE HOSPITAL
14. Royal Free London
16. Wait Outside
18. Driller Killer
20. Empty The Old Ashes

21. PET/MRI SCAN
22. Sitting In The Clinic
24. On The Edge

26. LYMPH GLAND CANCER
28. Smash Smash Smash
29. Needle Neck

32. Terrorist Cell (Operation Lymph)
34. Exhausted
36. Never Felt So Happy
38. After Stroke
40. Staple Lips
41. Sugar Tax
42. The Excited Result

44. CANCER CENTRE (RADIOTHERAPY)
46. Radio People
47. She Didn't Exit A Phone Box
48. CG1 ASTER Via Changing Room 3
50. Exhausted Again
52. Real Deal

54. NUCLEAR MEDICINE
56. Valley Of The Dinosaurs (Putting it mildly!)
58. Hip
60. Tuning Into Old Haunt
62. CCN (Iodine/Nuclear)
64. Enter The Big Brother House
66. Sweating
68. I Have Options
69. Pull, Glue, Smash And Out

70. Friday 4th February 2022
71. Night Off Cancers
72. March To March
73. No Record Of You (Royal Free)

74. OTHER TWISTS N TURNS
75. Great Uncle George Fuller, designer of the Richard Dimbleby Centre, Guys Hospital, meets the Duke of Edinburgh.
76. The Queen and Great Uncle George Fuller at the Richard Dimbleby Centre.
77. Mel meets one of her family, Petula Clark, during treatment.
78. Mel working on her radiation mask followed by images of her progress.
82. "REFLECTION" "FRIDA KAHLO INSPIRED MASK"
84. Special Thanks

DENTIST

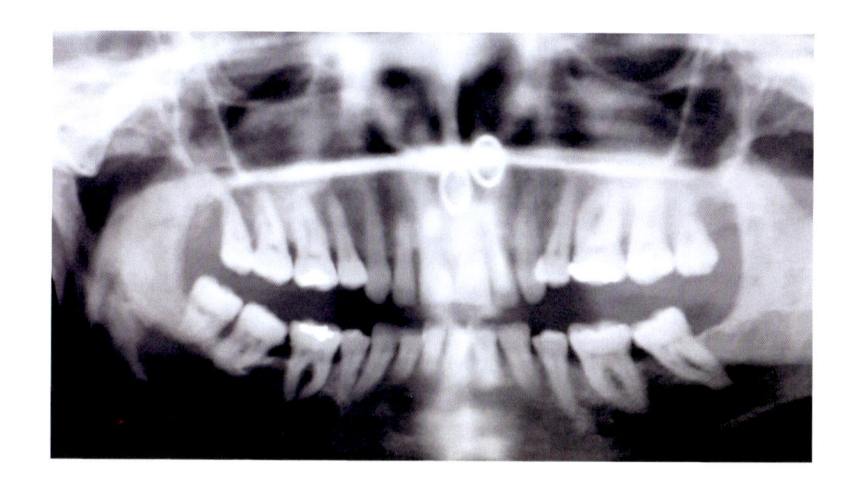

MENTAL DENTAL HEALTH

Mental dental hell

Dentist records inform?

Journey begins

Cancer, Amyloidosis, lymph gland n nodes

Radiotherapy, nuclear medicine

Chilled off, controlled with coconut ice drinks.

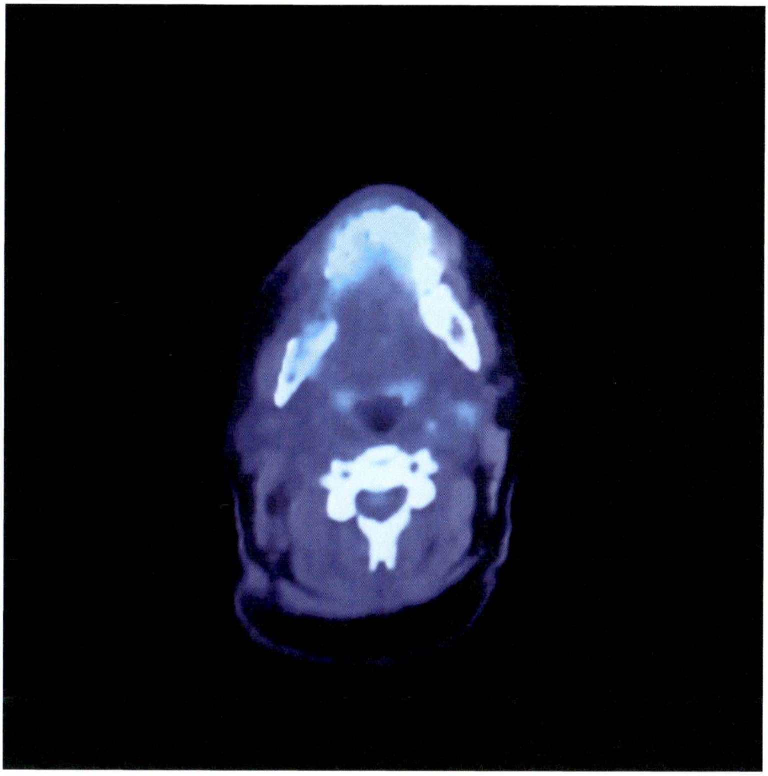

A Stranger's Wake Up Call

Deadly diseases and that thought pattern mix

Everything's intertwined, fate with/without fix

Dentist blessings in disguise, it was all meant to be?

Join the charity massive due to genes in family

People in the know. Weed you out and can tell?

Explain where your sitting, the view, the smell

Reel off your itinerary like a stalker, yet helps

Compassion leaves you in tears as a call about one thing becomes something else.

**Welcome to
the Cancer Centre at Guy's**

All patients please use self check-in on arrival

RADIOTHERAPY

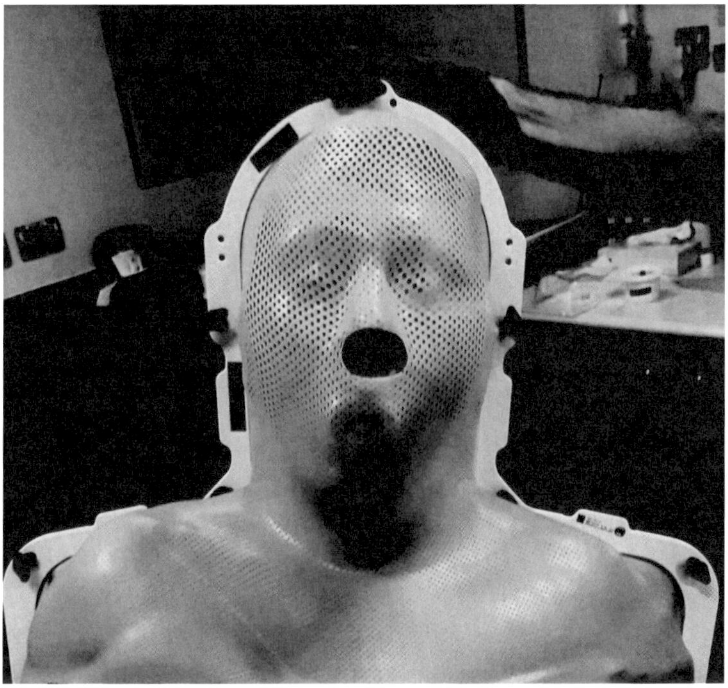

Mesh Mask For My Beautiful Angel

Leave the Clink museum

Walk into 2021

Whatever that means in my bloody head

God knows what it means to her?

Visions of, smelling the hell

Spin the morphine, spin the mouthwash

Cure is the word.

Avalanche, tsunami

Soaked from head to toe in possible death sentence.

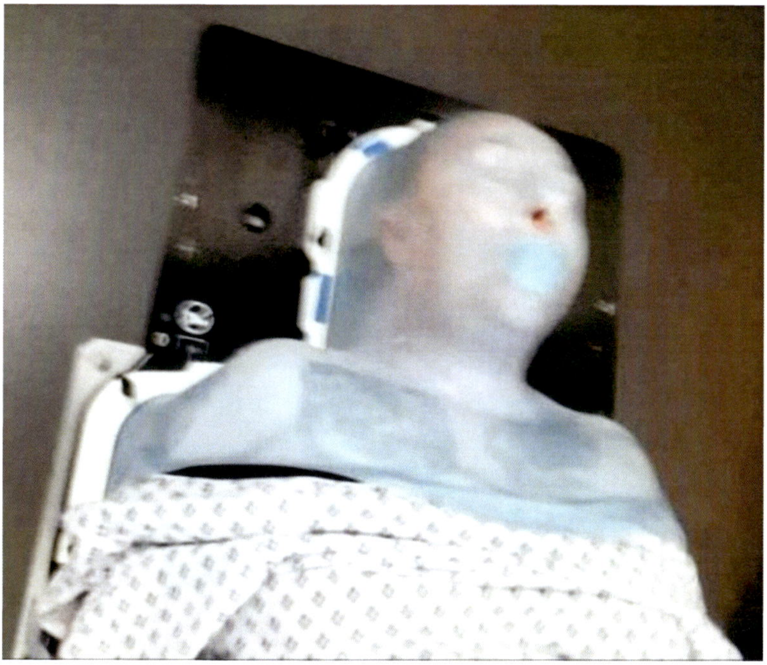

Swiss Extract

She had cancer and felt alone

I offered to go Swiss? She said no.

I tried to feel her pain? She explained how others would feel?

Bang goes my calm of bargaining, bang goes any deal.

Radiation Mesh Mask

Make appointment for a fitting

Wear over 5 weeks, 25 sittings

Flat plastic silhouette swims around developing style procedure

Melts down on face, snip holes around nose, mouth for breather

Take off the mask, meeting each Friday

Is it going to plan or bad news/bad day?

I watch several more brought into treatment

Everyone has been helped off the pavement

Going in for more? Another session for the weak?

Scares the hell out those still standing on our feet.

ROYAL FREE HOSPITAL

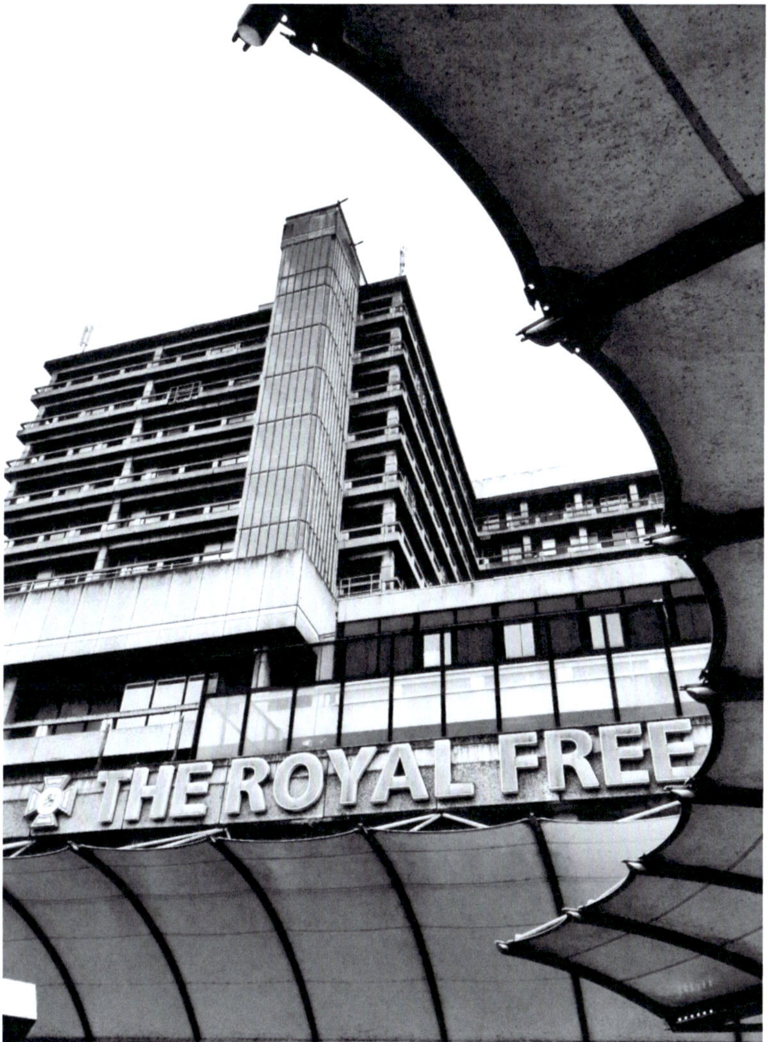
THE ROYAL FREE

Royal Free London

Take my other half to an hospital of many different era's

So strange and imposing, brings on one of my seizures

It's not my appointment, I'm here to cover her back

I confirm! I see what she sees, together we won't crack

Longest of corridors, longest of bends

Both our knees give way, no longer on mend

Walls and walls of "Thank you" cards

She gags on potassium, prevent thyroid shards

Another diving board into the abyss

Praying nothings found, praying nothings missed

Time to see consultant now scans are done?

Hello "Amyloidosis" or Cancer plus "One".

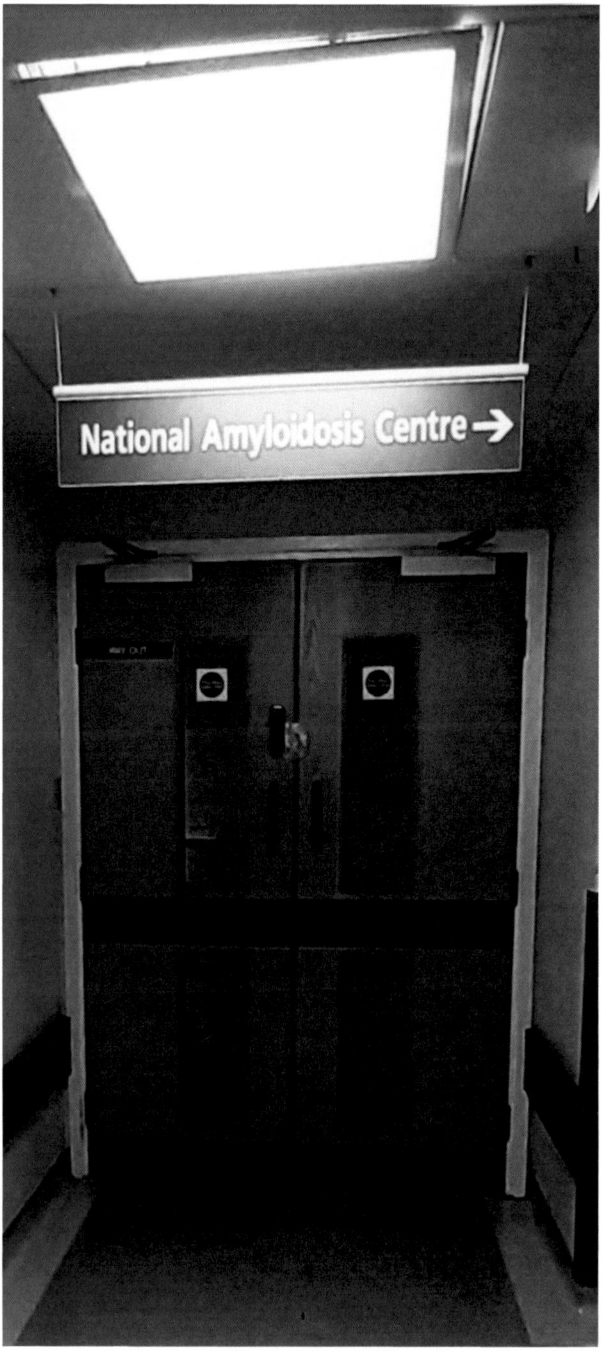
National Amyloidosis Centre

Wait Outside

Check enclosed map

Wait outside building, member of staff will collect you

Prepare for all day visit

Then be prepared to know nothing once again.

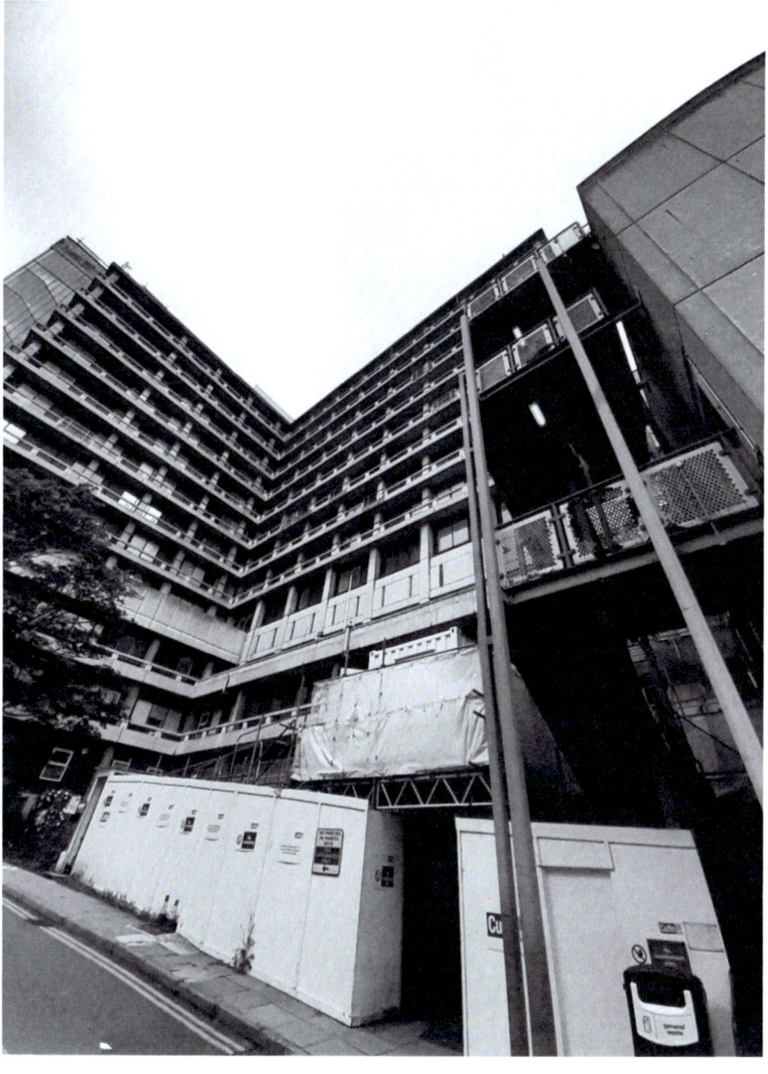

Driller Killer

The corkscrew unplugs a timeline

Prophetic yet pathetic

Impressed yet depressed

Neck needle nerve pain shoots from A-B

Bone Marrow routes clinics on the A-Z

Seems to prove I know nothing at all?

Umbrella illness or every clinic down the hall?

"Amyloidosis?"

I'm still reading up on that "Cancer" diagnosis?

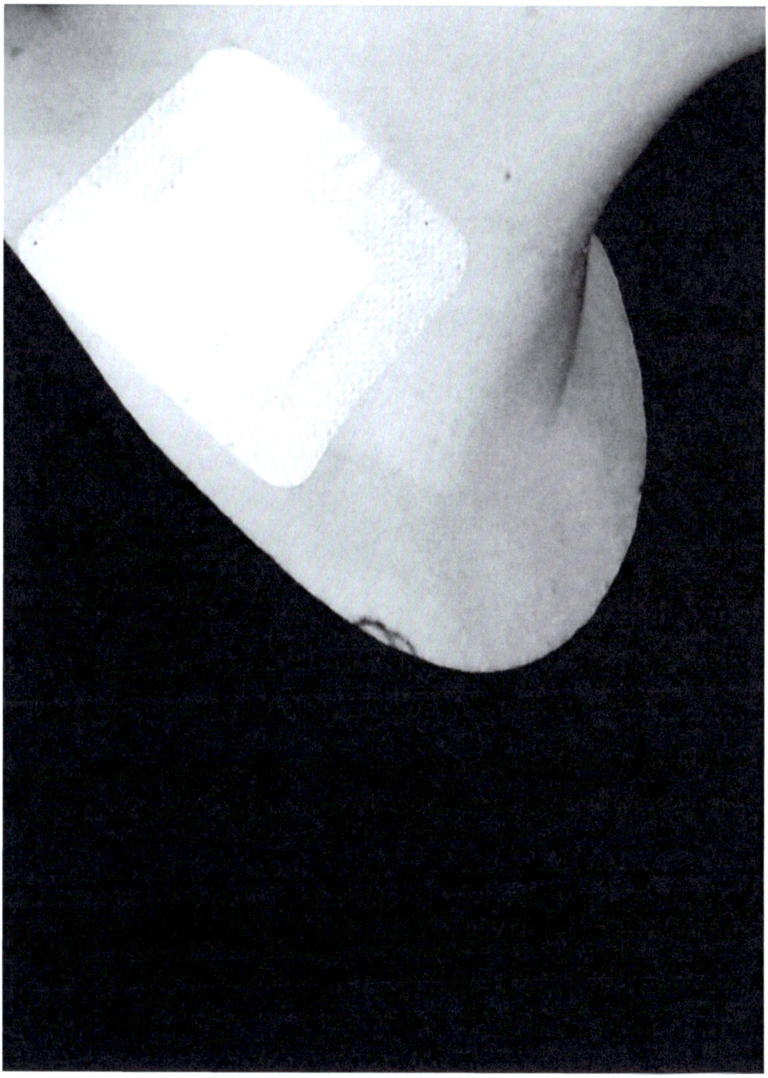

Empty The Old Ashes (Amyloidosis)

Pat on the back threw some light into this crusty rock hard block of suffering support and illness

Enough to spark a very strange spring of time consuming flows

Like a head injury? Unusual patterns, salty streams and swollen features

Again this is not for me. Cry, cry, cry it gets it out of system

You can feel relief to get up and start fresh, ready for next clinic.

PET/MRI SCAN

Sitting In The Clinic

MRI pet scan

All the terminology now applied

No longer numb, placed firmly inside

Know the corridors, units and how it all works

Talk quite frankly, comfort no longer lurks?

Hate the sound of laughter behind closed doors

Sounds too much like crying, guttural roars.

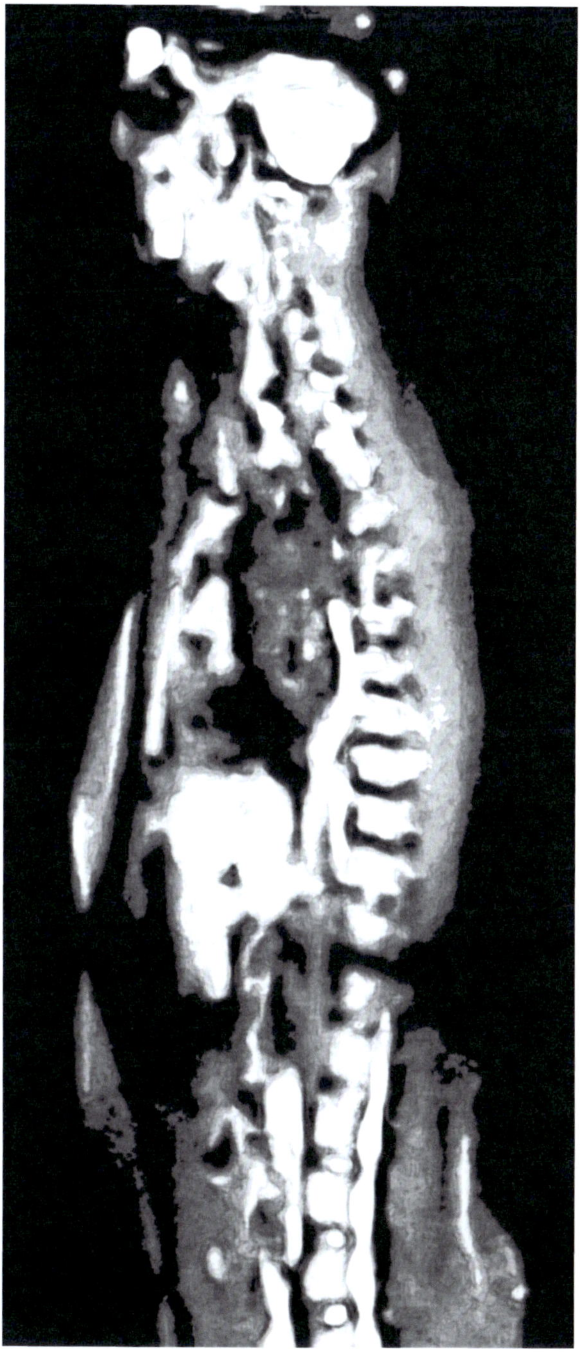

On The Edge

It's called the waiting game
Every day is worse

Exhausted after random thoughts, then into room, the real victim bursts

Emotional temper, emotional apologies, emotional dealing with death

Can't reassure a person in agony who can hardly draw their breath

What the hell do I know anyway? I'm not some higher power

Unlike this bastard that's got us gripped, ready to devour.

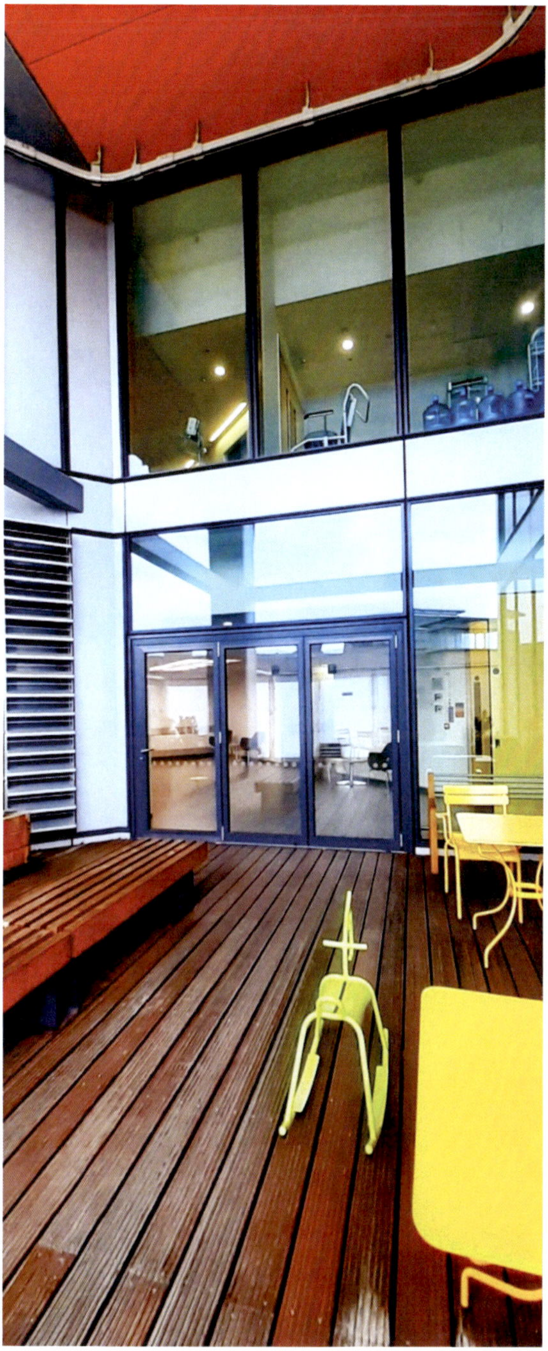

LYMPH GLAND CANCER

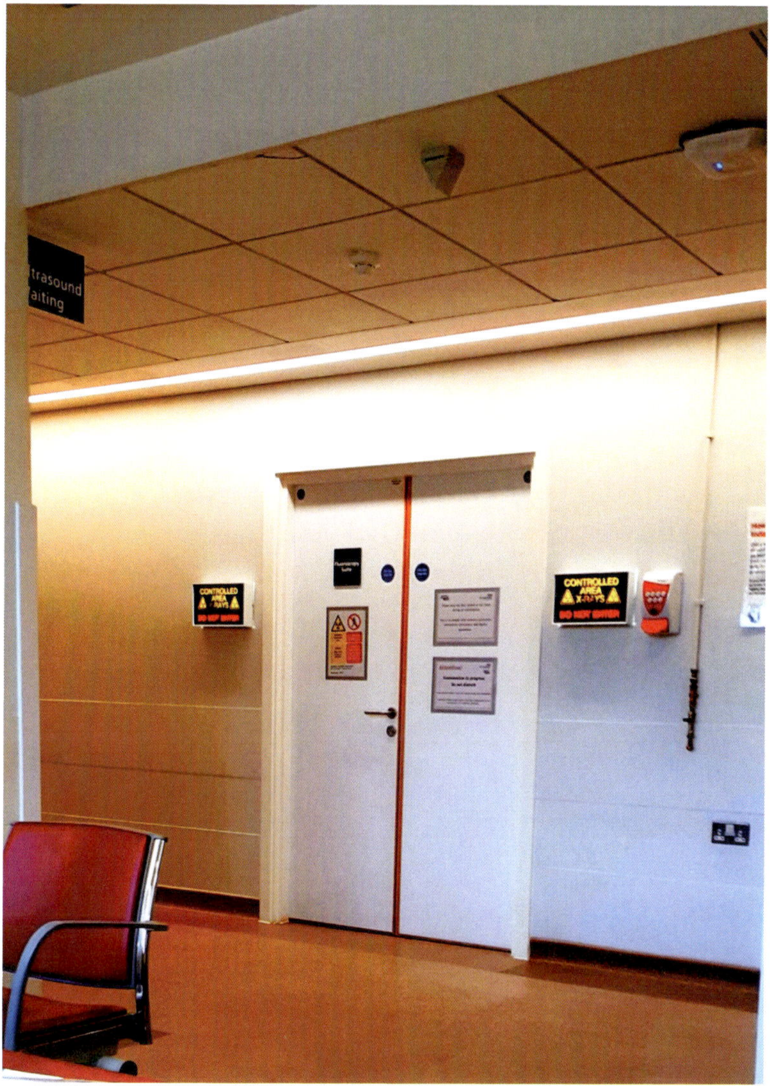
trasound
aiting
CONTROLLED
AREA
X-RAYS
DO NOT ENTER

Smash Smash Smash

Cancel radiotherapy she has a bigger problem now

"It's not about that cancer? It's a new type that we've found"

Thyroid to the lymph gland it's also very rare?

Forget the Amyloidosis? This is more urgent to be fair

New team will contact you start treatment in one week

Now go and have a nice drink and take the weight off your feet.

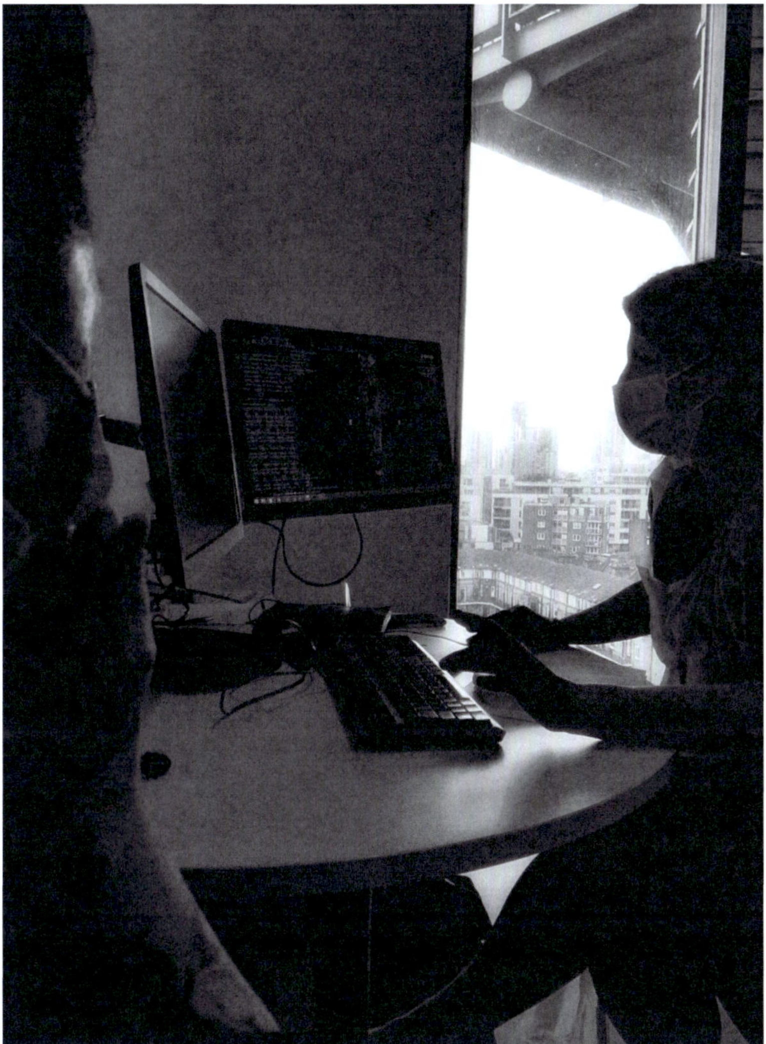

Needle Neck

Blue dye and pet scan

Have the treatments worked?

Back next month to hear final score?

The blitz of Head, neck and throat

Removal & co

Feeling low

Campaign to keep sanity?

Routines of pleasure

Coffee, cakes, views

Sugary drinks, an ongoing drug.

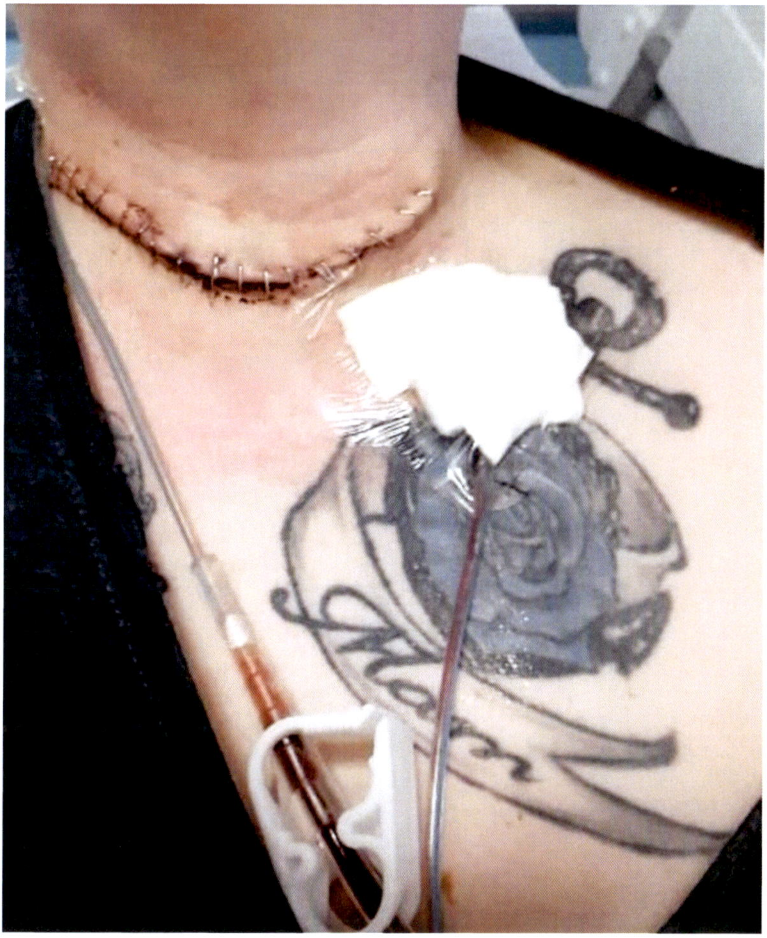

Terrorist Cell (Operation Lymph)

Removed by expert

Luckily poisons sucked before collapse

Although trail of damage leaves young

Back again it angles her shoulder, slithering down chest

Strangling neck

Removed once again, the damage mounts

Takes its toll

Sweating day and night

Hallucinations

Fears, terror and tears

Snatching bite grabs chin

More fighting

More pull than ever

Species recorded

Added to emergency surgery

It isn't giving up???

It reappears like personal devil

Sly serpent

Spreading hell.

33

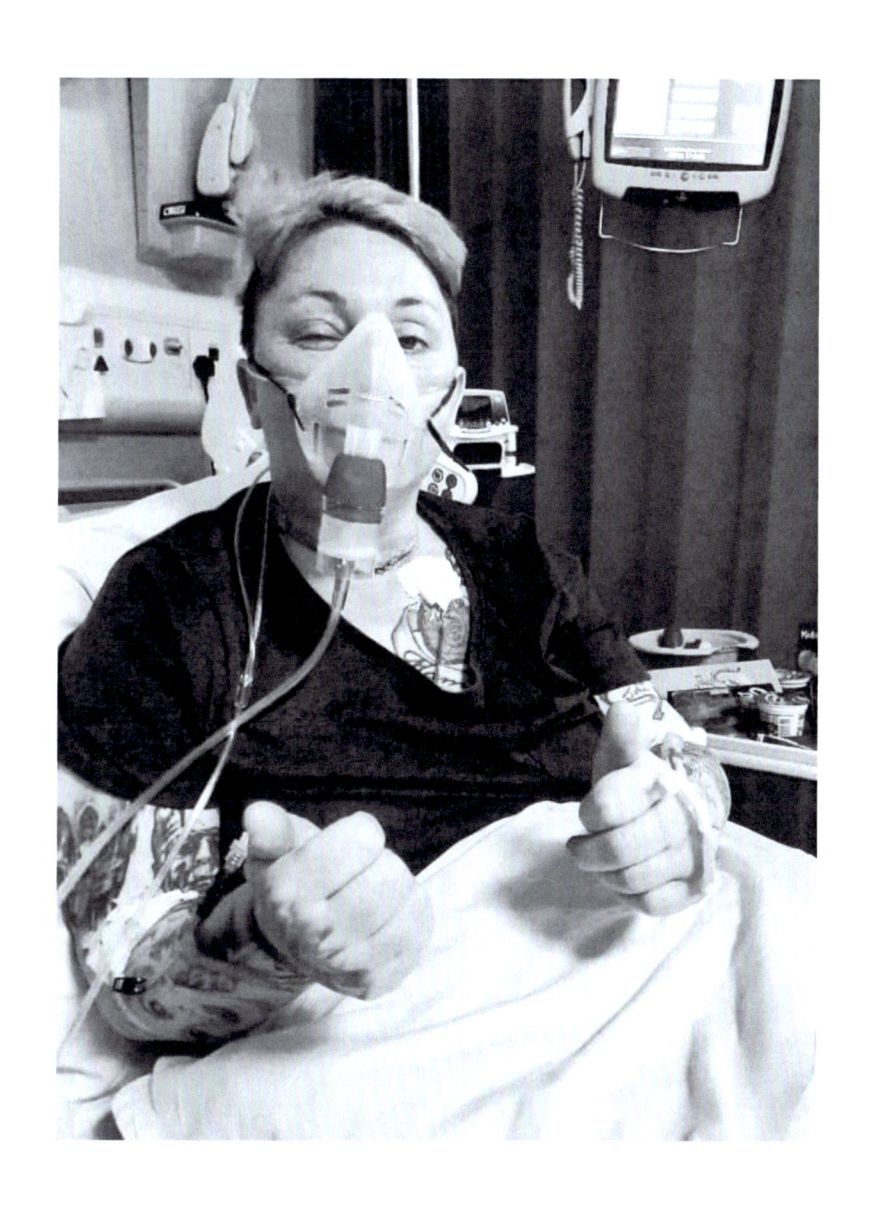

Exhausted

Beat to seat

Ratty feet

Ten minutes standing

Too demanding

Then straight to desk n chair

Don't care about glares for being unfair

Priority seating

Means they're slow and beaten

Ignored falls and screams

Push and shove at full steam.

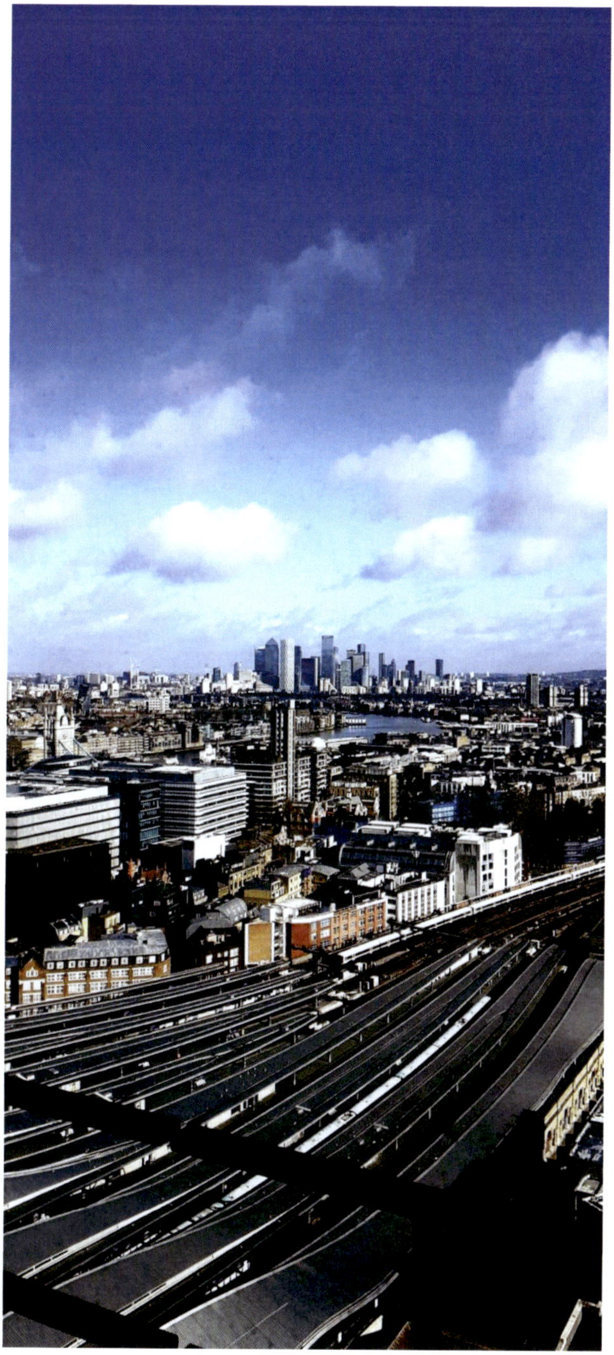

Never Felt So Happy

Happy happy happy lymphoma

Never felt so happy to have a loved ones throat slit?

Biopsies leave her hoarse, so dry, no spit

Remove the thyroid, remove the lymph nodes

Life of Iodine! That means there is a road?

What else can I worry about? As I've got so much to worry about?

Will her voice remain the same?

Whisper? Shout?

Just survive

Leave recovery alive.

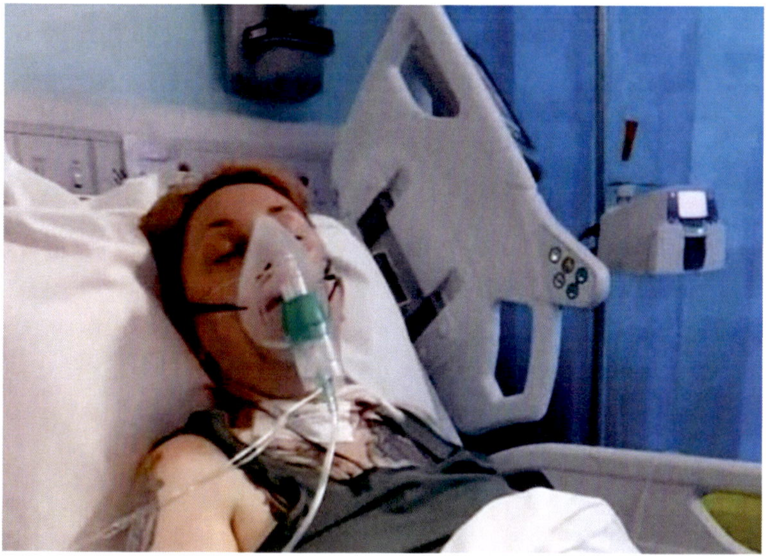

After Stroke

Unstitch, Pull out your drains

Clean the staples, flush your veins

Ready for your daily steps

Down corridor then a little to left

Fragile lady? I hold your hand

Back to oxygen, nebulizer, ventolin and fans

The walk to build strength

Shows the truth in stay length

I call the ward later there is confusion a blur

You're being rushed to King's Hospital as speech was a slur

Suspected stroke? I'm kept well away?

Negative? Back to your old hospital bed, Positive she stays.

Ruskin 5 Floor

Friends Stroke Unit →

5 Floor

Staple Lips

Who said life was a bed of Roses?

Maybe your smile's an ailment of your diagnosis?

Sugar Tax

Had to drop the sugar when diagnosed with diabetes

6am, fizzy drink and one large bag of sweeties

The image dangles in my head. That purchase at the station

Another two more when we reach destination

Now the drug of choice! rewarding it gets job done

Need 5 teeth out when there's gap in her treatment as all I feel are crumbs!

But a fix to fix was all I asked? Cross other bridges later

Sweetheart needs the world to keep spinning whilst in and out of theatre.

The Excited Result

You're home, at last lay down your head

I then run and jump in pre op bed

They knock me out and cut me up

I return back home, morphine we sup

Your throat is stapled and I am still bleeding

No rest for the wicked, the cats need feeding

While we are awake we do what we can

Are we allowed meals on wheels? Joking?
Yeah course I am.

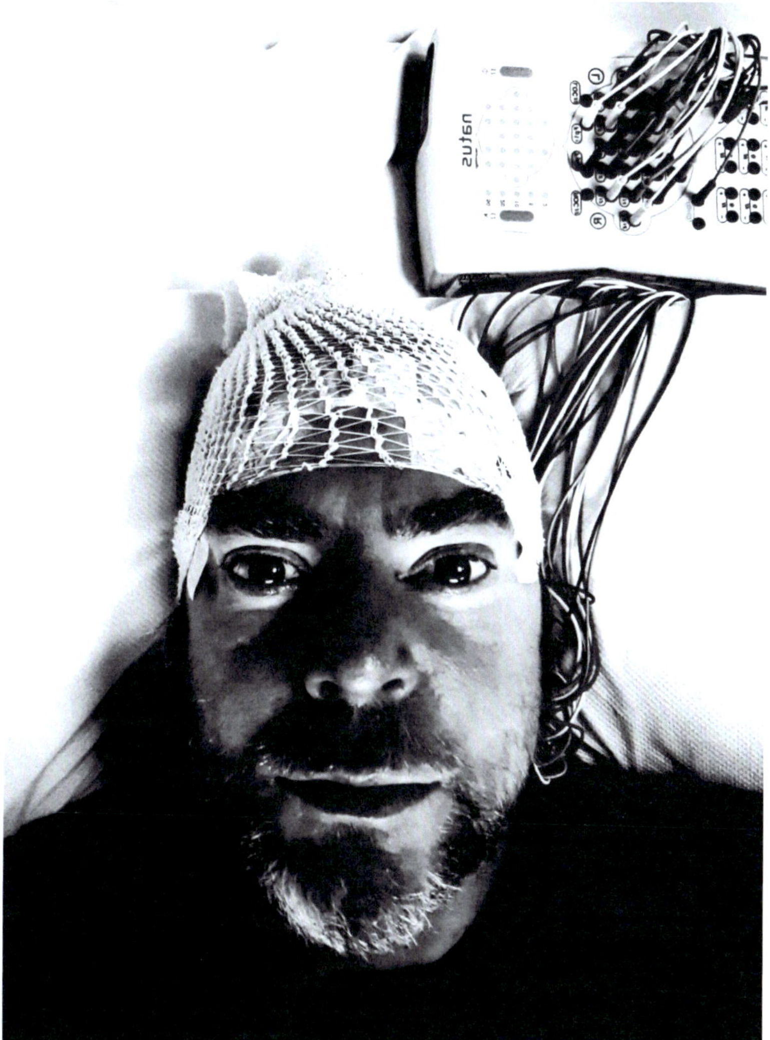
natus

CANCER CENTRE (RADIOTHERAPY)

Guy's Cancer

NHS

Appointments for: Ms Melanie Griffiths

Hospital Number: 6326264N
NHS Number: 4966982960

Day/Date	Time	Description	Location
Mon, September 13, 2021	10:15 am	Radiotherapy	G1 Aster
Tue, September 14, 2021	8:30 am	Radiotherapy	G5 Iris
Wed, September 15, 2021	11:15 am	Radiotherapy	G5 Iris
Thu, September 16, 2021	8:55 am		G1 Aster
Fri, September 17, 2021	10:05 am		G2 Buttercup
Mon, September 20, 2021	10:00 am		G1 Aster
Tue, September 21, 2021	10:00 am		G1 Aster
Wed, September 22, 2021	10:00 am		G1 Aster
Thu, September 23, 2021	10:00 am		G1 Aster
Fri, September 24, 2021	10:00 am		G1 Aster
Mon, September 27, 2021	10:00 am		G1 Aster
Tue, September 28, 2021	10:00 am		G1 Aster
Wed, September 29, 2021	10:05 am		G1 Aster
Thu, September 30, 2021	10:00 am		G1 Aster
Fri, October 1, 2021	10:05 am		G1 Aster
Mon, October 4, 2021	10:00 am		G1 Aster
Tue, October 5, 2021	10:30 am		G5 Iris
Wed, October 6, 2021	10:15 am		G5 Iris
Thu, October 7, 2021	10:45 am		G1 Aster
Fri, October 8, 2021	9:15 am		G5 Iris
Mon, October 11, 2021	10:00 am		G1 Aster
Tue, October 12, 2021	10:00 am		G1 Aster
Wed, October 13, 2021	10:00 am		G1 Aster

These are your scheduled appointment(s), however please be aware that these times may be subject to change due to unavoidable circumstances

Radio People

Radio stars

The world is on the radio

It's a weird weird life on the radio

People are sick on the radio

I am scared and sick watching the radio.

SHE DIDN'T EXIT A PHONE BOX?

Never seen another person look as ill

Apart from heads down toilets usually pints and pills

She was guided from an ambulance with a bowl and red eyes

Got out of her way you know how things can fly?

I said "She needs a rest and the best of care?"

My partner stated the reason why she was going in there?

Another round of radiotherapy was on the menu

From the kindest, cruellest, craziest painful of venues.

CG1 ASTER VIA CHANGING ROOM 3

Name shows on screen
Nobody greets, nobody meets
Enter changing room 3
Gowned, tied, emotional
Leave through a backdoor
To a different room
With personal machine
Sit on chair alone in eerie space
Silence
Waiting for contact with somebody
Then taken to table
Reunited with mesh mask
Mirror image staring back
A snake or rock
It bolts down body
Music plays
A circle performed twice
Bed lowered down back to earth
Exit via entered door to another world.

49

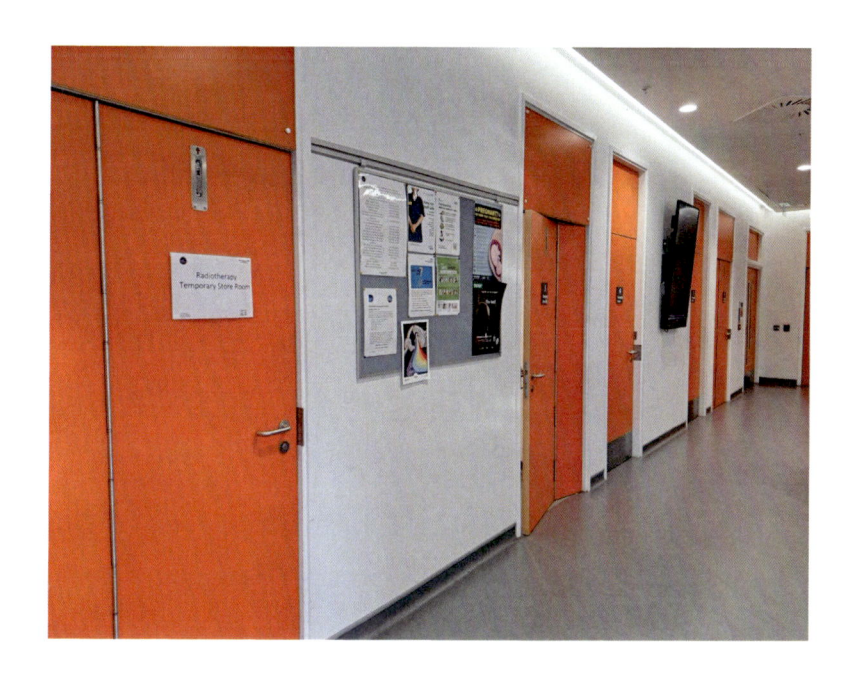

Exhausted Again

Whimpering mother/gran wheeled to changing room

Starts wave of emotions
Tears, heavy breathing, some leave waiting area

There's clearly Genes in this familiar story

Devastating flashbacks, five rows of reactions

No thought of personal struggle just loved ones who have gone

Yet nowhere to escape, look to waiting board your name is now on.

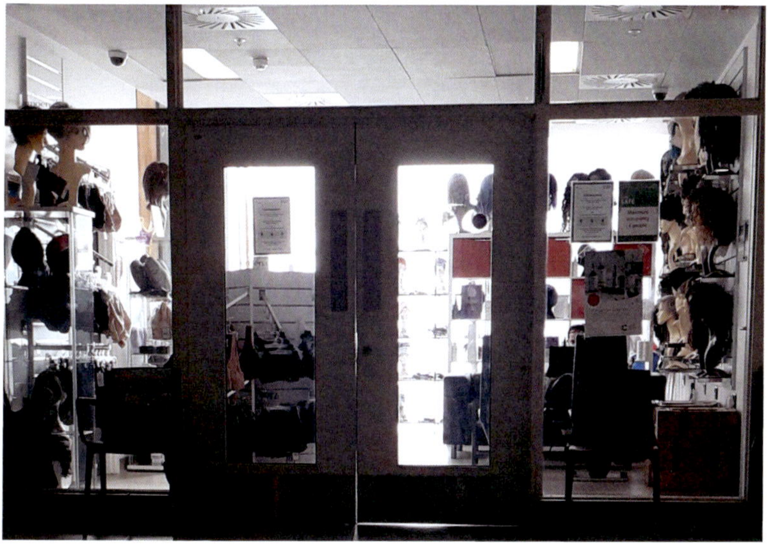

Real Deal

Get angry reading about rock n roll bands

A mid life crises, pout or horned shaped hands

Usual site under the light

Perhaps I'm used to danger?

Partner's cancer fight?

25th treatment day

Keep your mesh mask, heavy price to pay

You say for now and I know you may be right

We know nothing of the cancer snake? With several million style of bites.

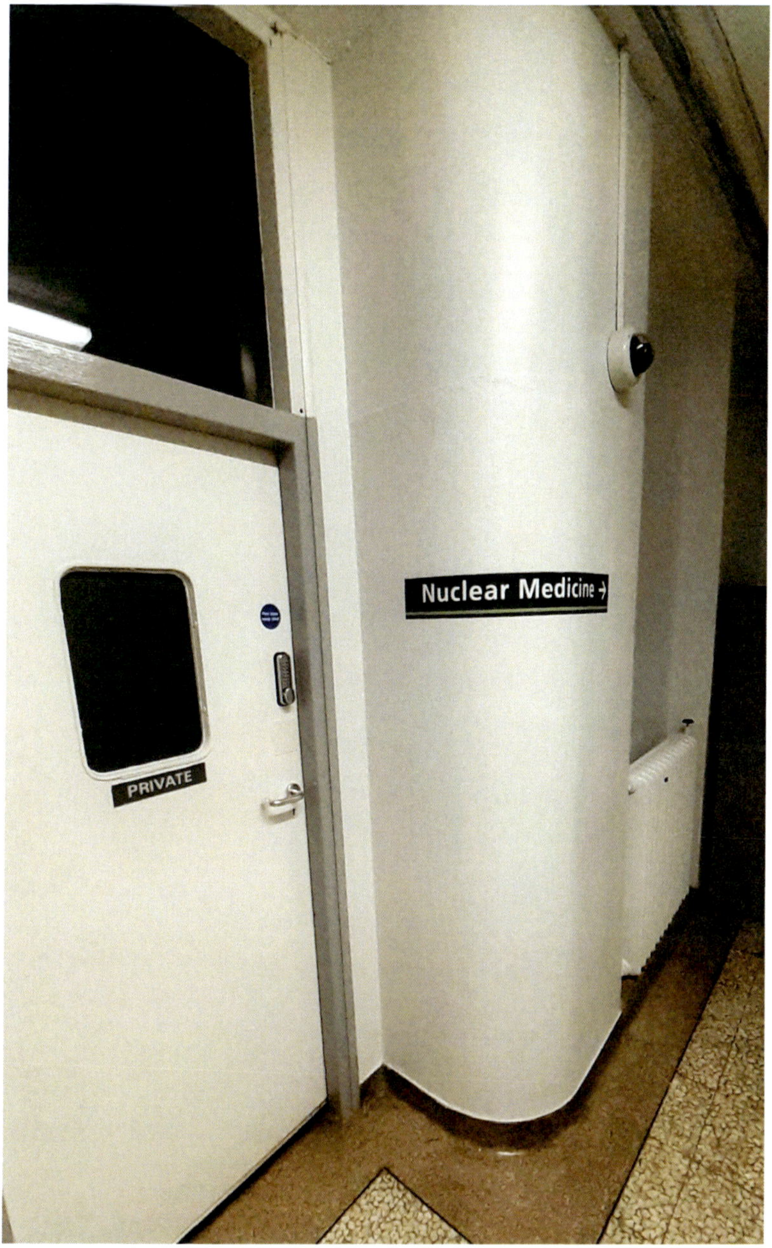
Nuclear Medicine →
PRIVATE

NUCLEAR MEDICINE

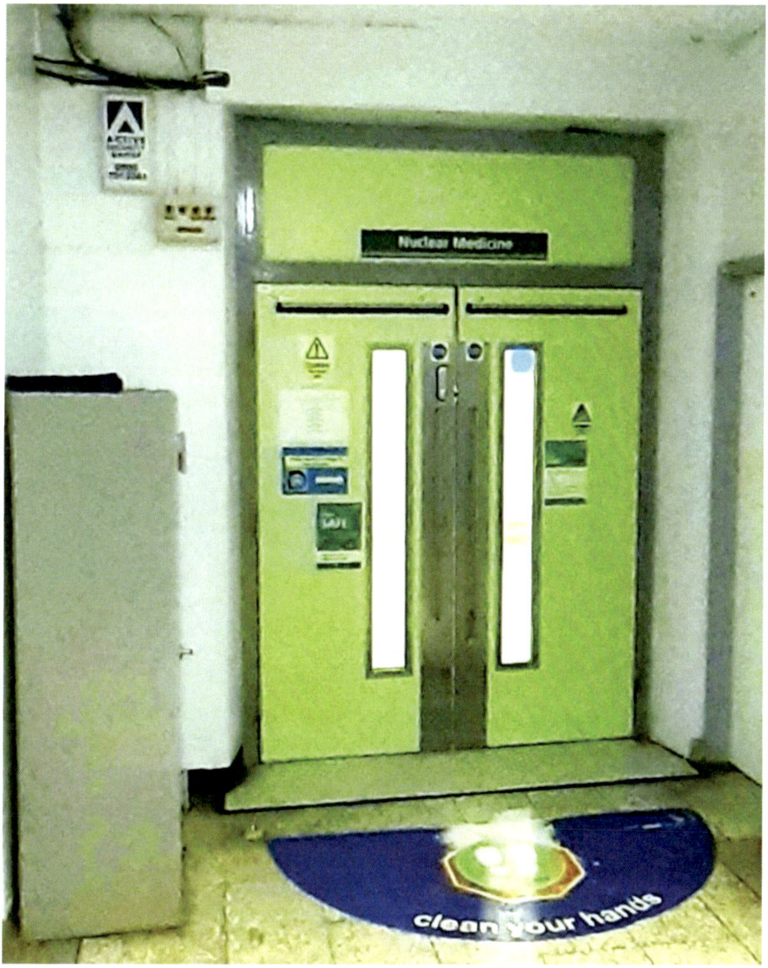

Nuclear Medicine
clean your hands

VALLEY OF THE DINOSAURS (Putting It Mildly!)

She deals with dying, I deal with loss

One stays in our lounge, the other? Off

No longer the star when following the hearse

Nobody's tears left, If your last not first.

57

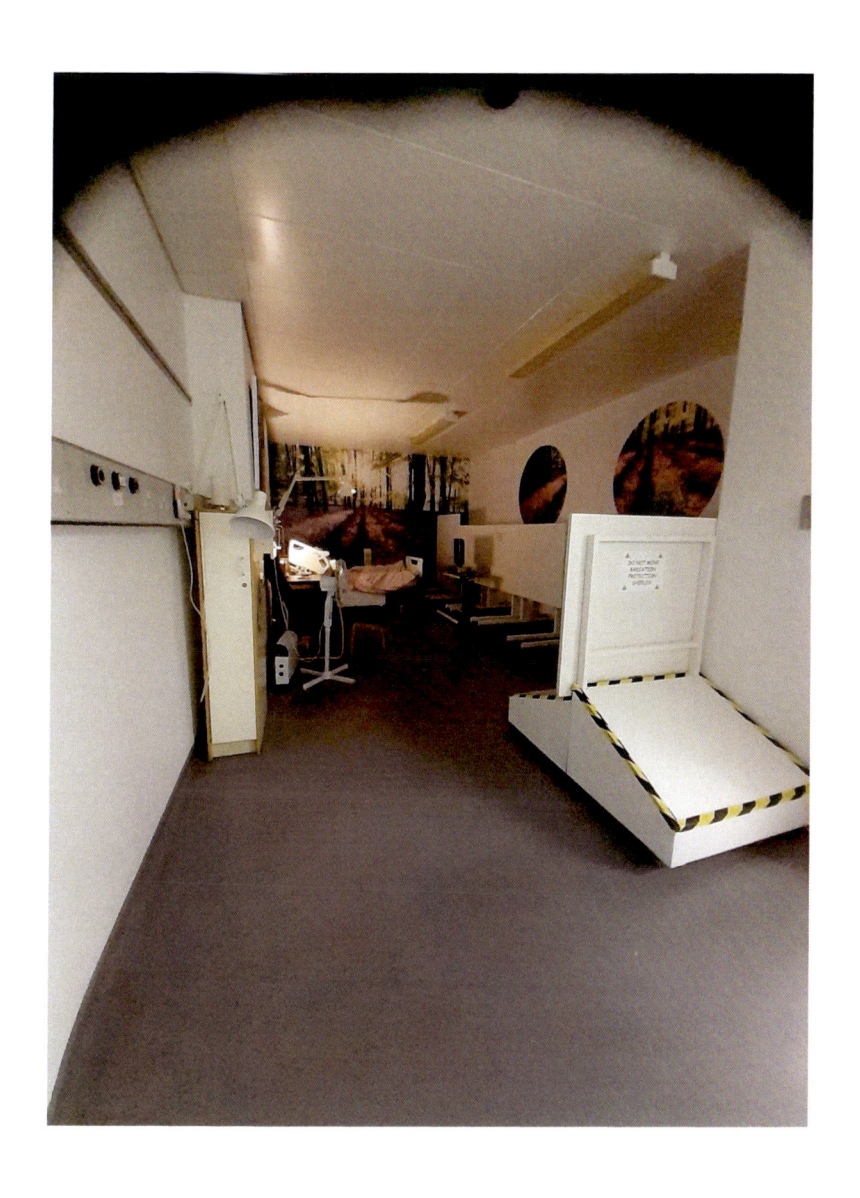

HIP

Away at first break.

Together again illness our hard make

Now we go to battle, our experience blends for war

Craters of cancer don't know the hell in store

Like a creepy poltergeist ready to attack

Doesn't expect one almighty smack.

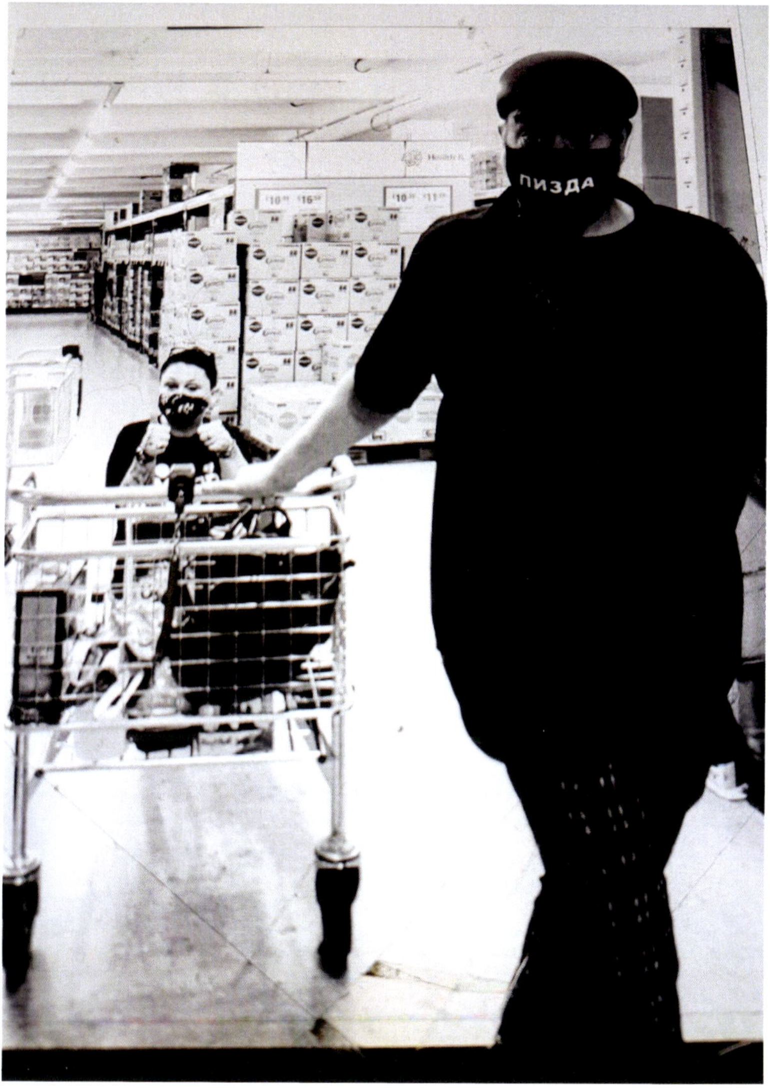
ПИЗДА

Tuning Into Old Haunt

I'll die of stress than runaway from my chosen life

Not a professional coward that seeks room with every mess up

My ears may burn? We know the pitch of the idle!

You shiver, I'm walking on your grave, living once again, next to death.

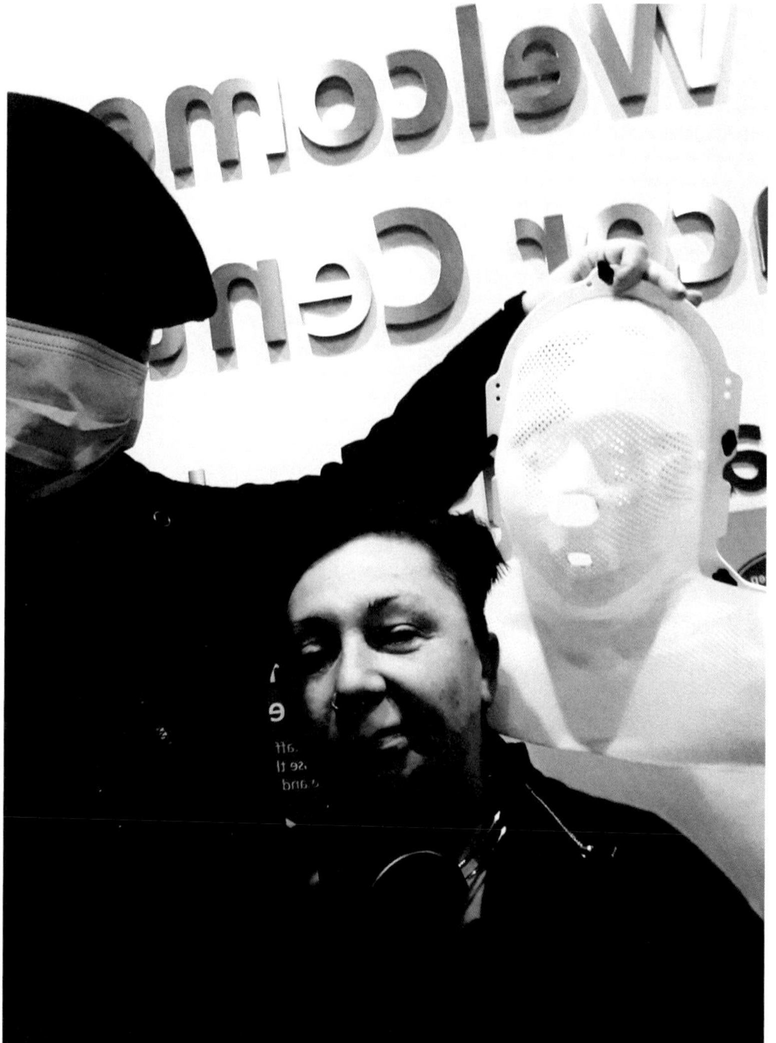

CCN (Iodine/Nuclear)

Here comes the Community cancer nurse with the first injection of two

Job done

I grab the packed bag of my partner ready for the Cancer big brother house stay

Observations of iodine treatment in a hospital "Pad" with shared kitchen and bathroom?

When home we have separate rooms for 2 weeks

Body of iodine Radiation allows a short hug before cats and myself traipse to room down hall.

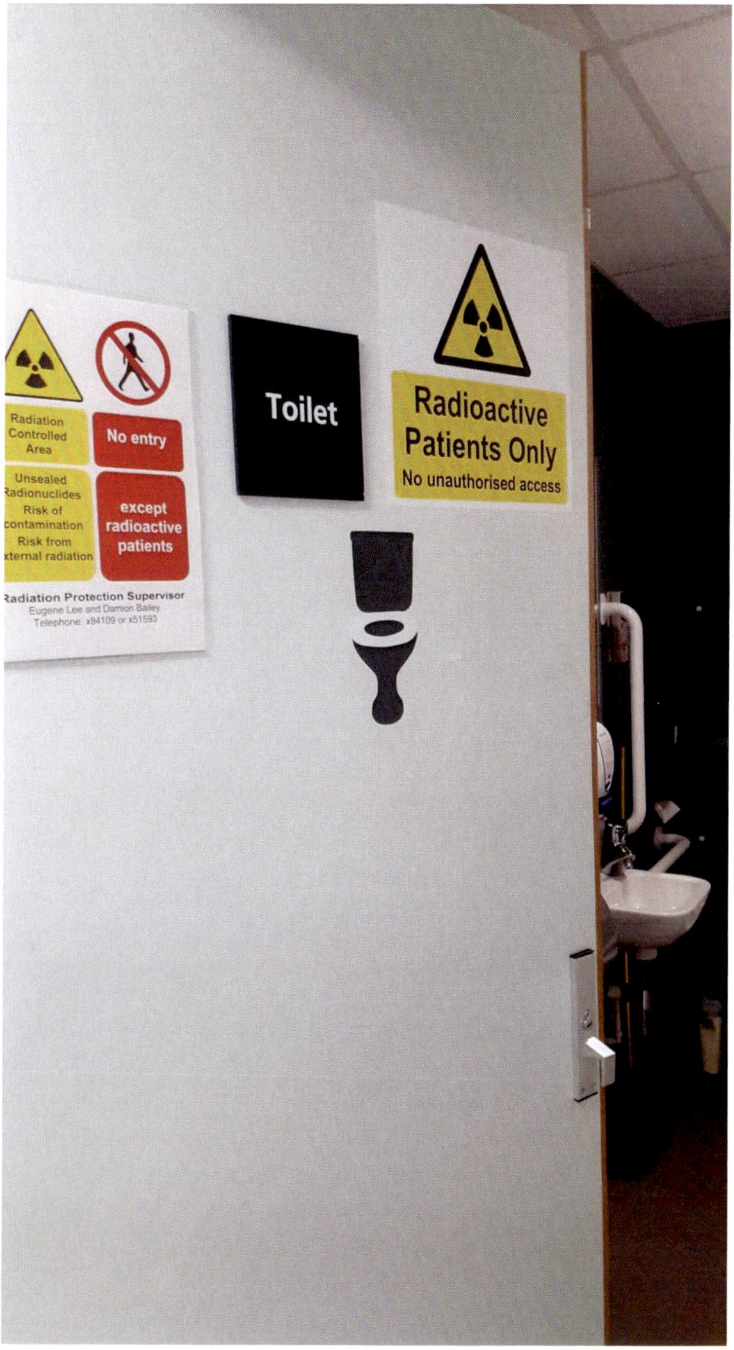
Radiation Controlled Area
No entry
Unsealed
adionuclides
Risk of
contamination
Risk from
xternal radiation
except radioactive patients
adiation Protection Supervisor
Eugene Lee and Damion Bailey
Telephone: x84109 or x51593
Toilet
Radioactive Patients Only
No unauthorised access

Enter The Big Brother House

Stand behind radioactive protective shields

Can't touch, go anywhere the one I love

She faces the CCTV

Can hear a pin drop in this empty quarter

The doctor delivered that powerful pill

From one test tube into another onto her tongue

Radiation suit leaves and locks the door

Now the worry of side effects really starts

A Japanese woman appears from nowhere patient 2 of 2 for the passing of info

Back to rooms, family on zoom never know what to say?

Plenty of water, plenty of magazines, plenty of rest say those up all night worrying

Spend a fortune on gifts for the one I miss for now not Xmas.

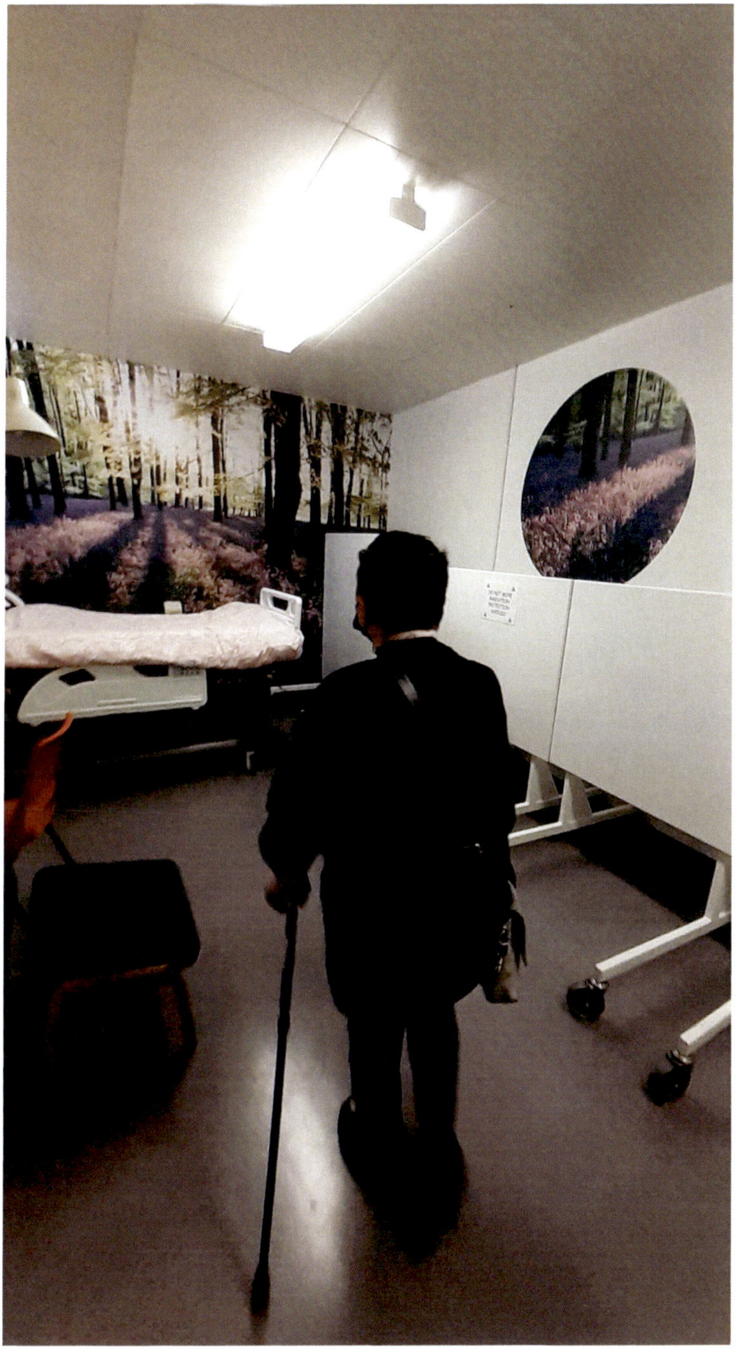

Sweating

Head, hands cooking

Eczema under breasts, groin, split skin

Sky high BP rate 154/120 second pneumonia and flu jab

Trouble passing water

Mouth is bleeding and in pain

Headaches, migraines

New pain, back of neck, shoulder blade and below

Diarrhoea after anything ate, liquids only, energy is low.

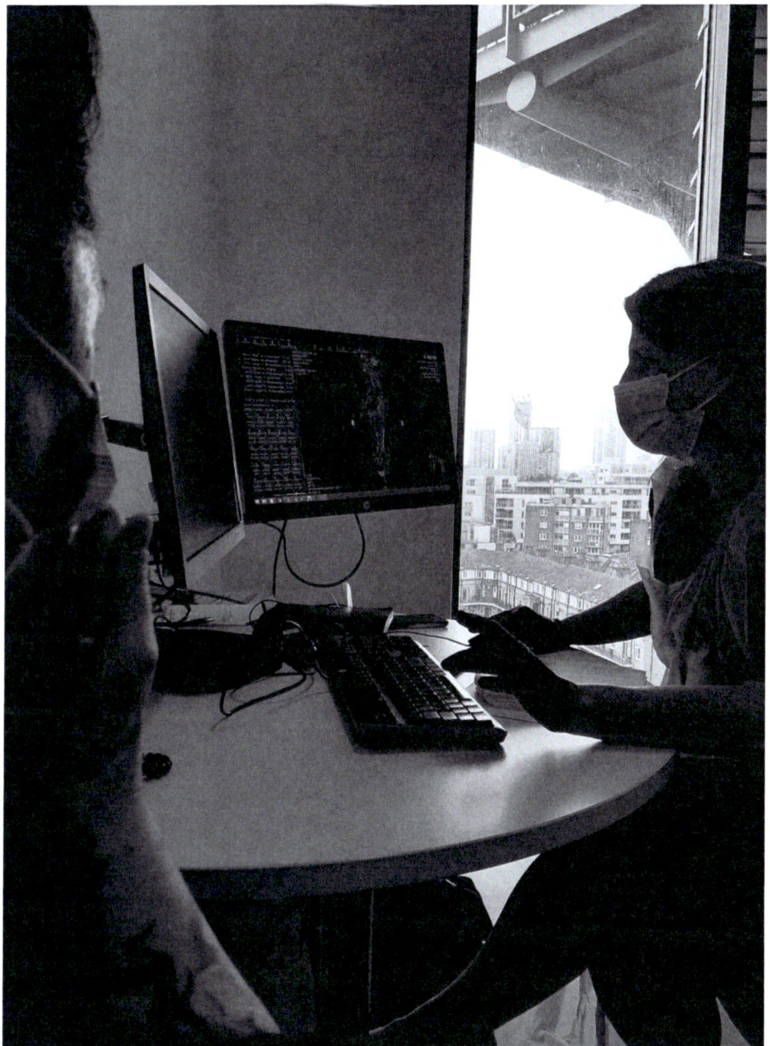

I Have Options

When the nurse drains her veins

I go home and think? One day I may try the same.

Pull, Glue, Smash And Out

Break in her treatment you know what that means
My turn to go under knife from crohns to epilepsy
5 teeth plucked due to grinding seizures
Ulcers, blood loss and gastro fears
All got too much grand mal attack in theatre
No longer a shock as I'm told much later?
Just recover. Lie low, no time to waste
Her final results of all the battles soon we shall face.

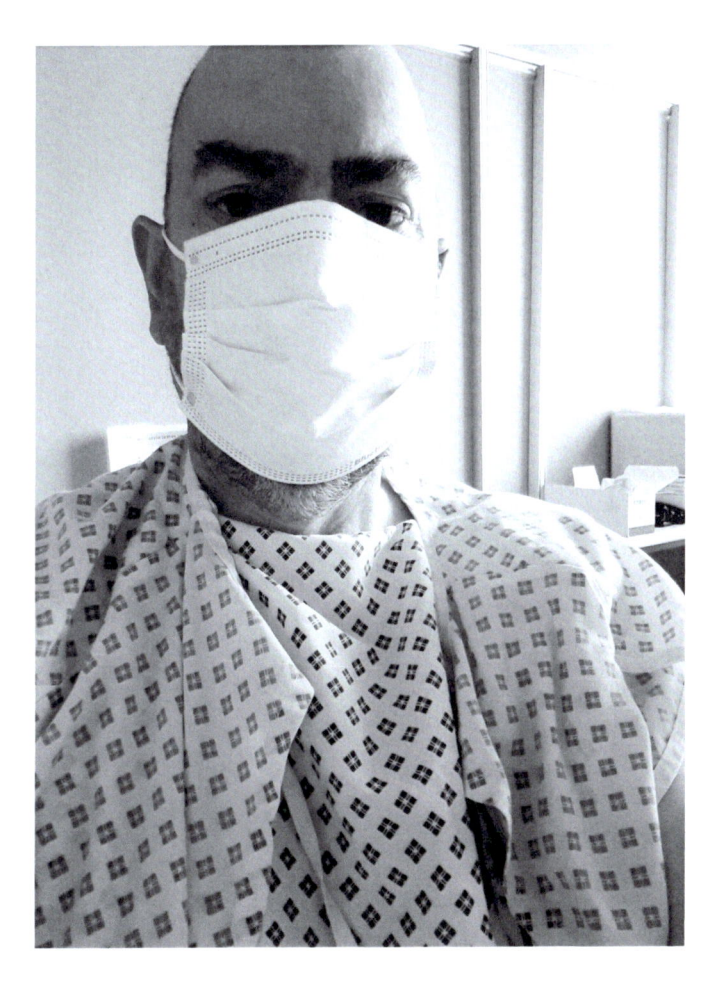

Friday 4th February 2022

Been a trip? waiting for "Spread or glory?"
Results in a golden envelope?

The imagined long trek, waiting room
Jitters, e roll call, knock & enter and then?

Nothing of the sort? Working from home with flu of the year!

"THE PHONE CALL" the heroic doctor. Marathon today work in the morning!

With the strongest WW2 jolly accent a young doctor could spring?

"Oh silly me! I'm so busy explaining possibility of gallstones I didn't explain results that clearly!

Yes you're 100% cancer free! ...ohhh you poor thing have a good cry it's ok!....YOU'RE OK?"

Night Off Cancers

Need a night off cancers plus own illnesses
So have rare trip to the Entertainment businesses
Most close at nine or ten
Worse of the worse left open then
Within the hour I'm explaining behaviour
Outnumbered four to one, no bouncers, no saviour
Night of shouting, edgy back glances
No dances, romances, just coked up trances
A night down the funnel
Chased and battered down the foot tunnel.

March To March!

Crohns, epilepsy and depression has zapped every ounce of life left

Apologise for zero energy, unable to attend

The first appointment I'm unable to support you
So I wait at home for the results from hell

Contemplating that type of future that doubt prepares

The cats' ears spring up, your steps are so well known!

Key in the door, I feel sick and want to bury head in sand

Look up, lights switched to the biggest of wild smiles!

Blood is clear, no cancer in body, surreal as it started, in shock what the hell?!!!

Ring a bell? Ring a bell?!!

No Record Of You (Royal Free)

2&2 = A punch out of blue.

A follow up. Done via referral?

In system. So why back to GP?

Back to beginning? No records to show?

Looking online for Royal Free London Amyloidosis clinic/secretary anybody?

Spot "4 -7 yrs life expectancy after diagnosis?"

Penny drops or something I remember.
"If you're still alive give us a shout or assumed dead?"

OTHER TWISTS N TURNS

Great Uncle George Fuller, designer of the Richard Dimbleby Centre, Guys Hospital, meets the Duke of Edinburgh.

The Queen and Great Uncle George Fuller at the Richard Dimbleby Centre.

Mel meets one of her family, Petula Clark, during treatment.

Mel working on her radiation mask.

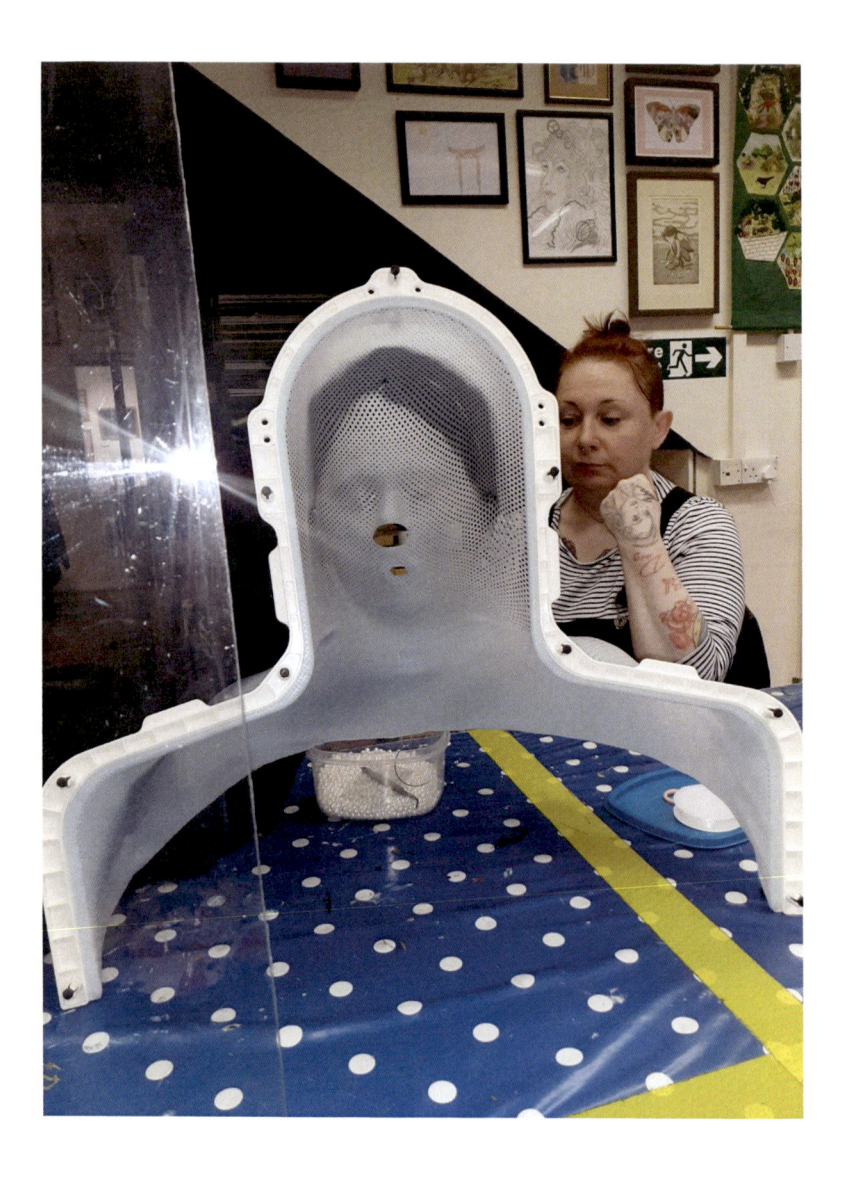

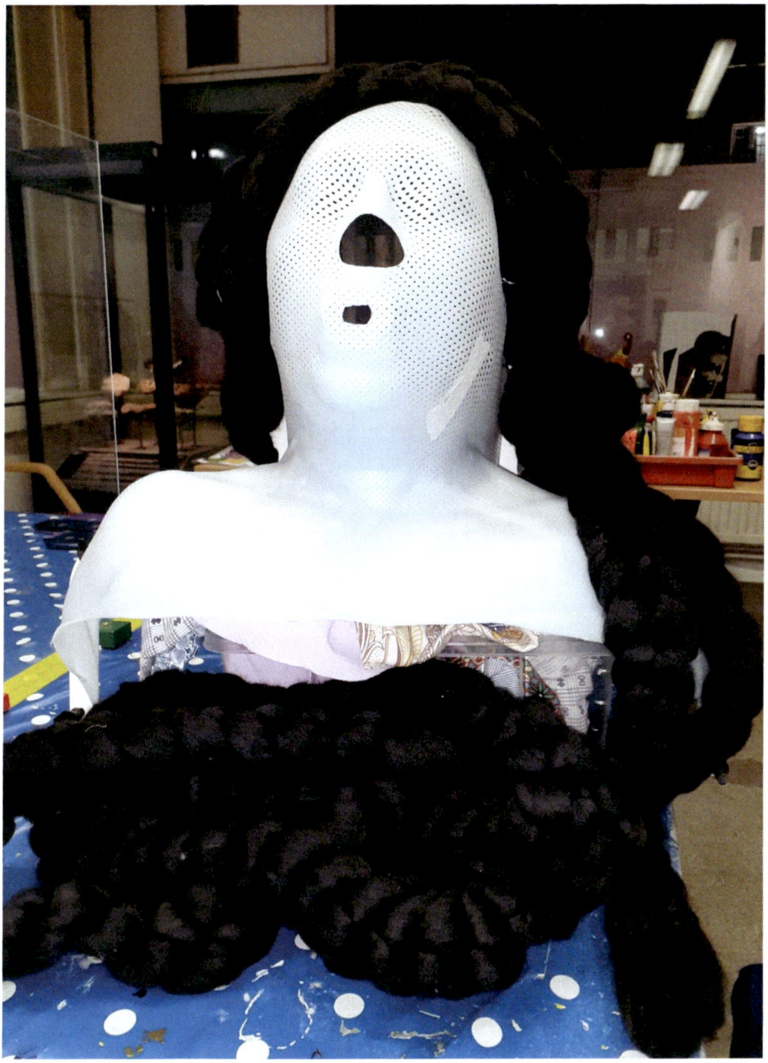

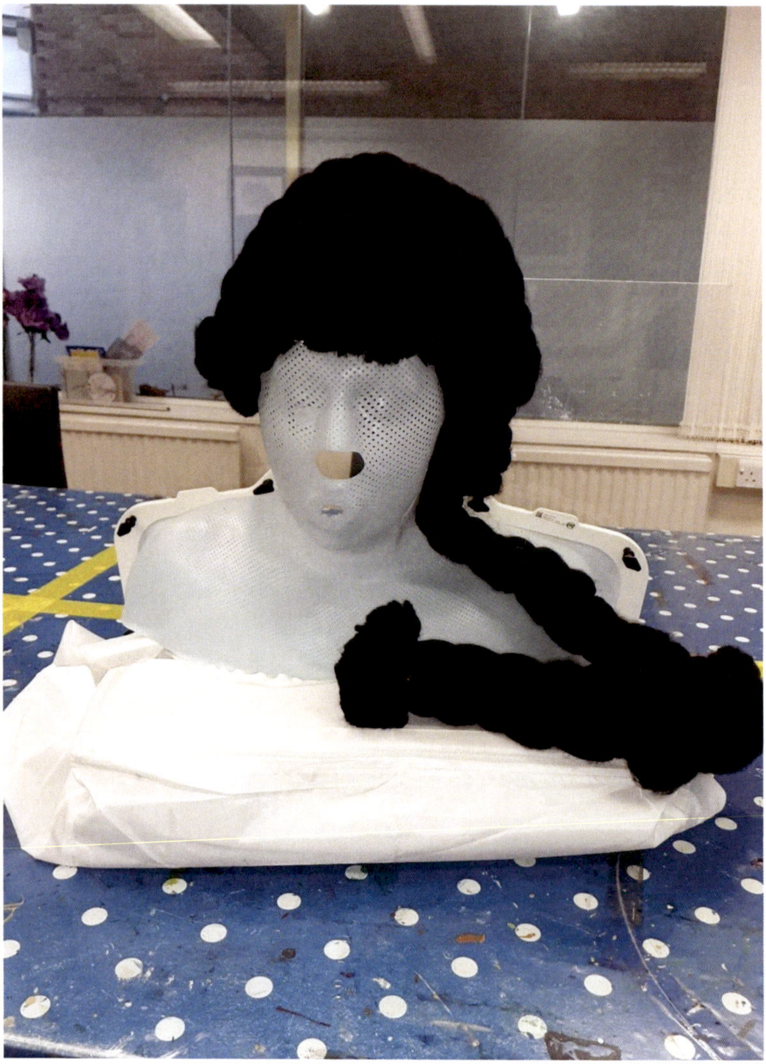

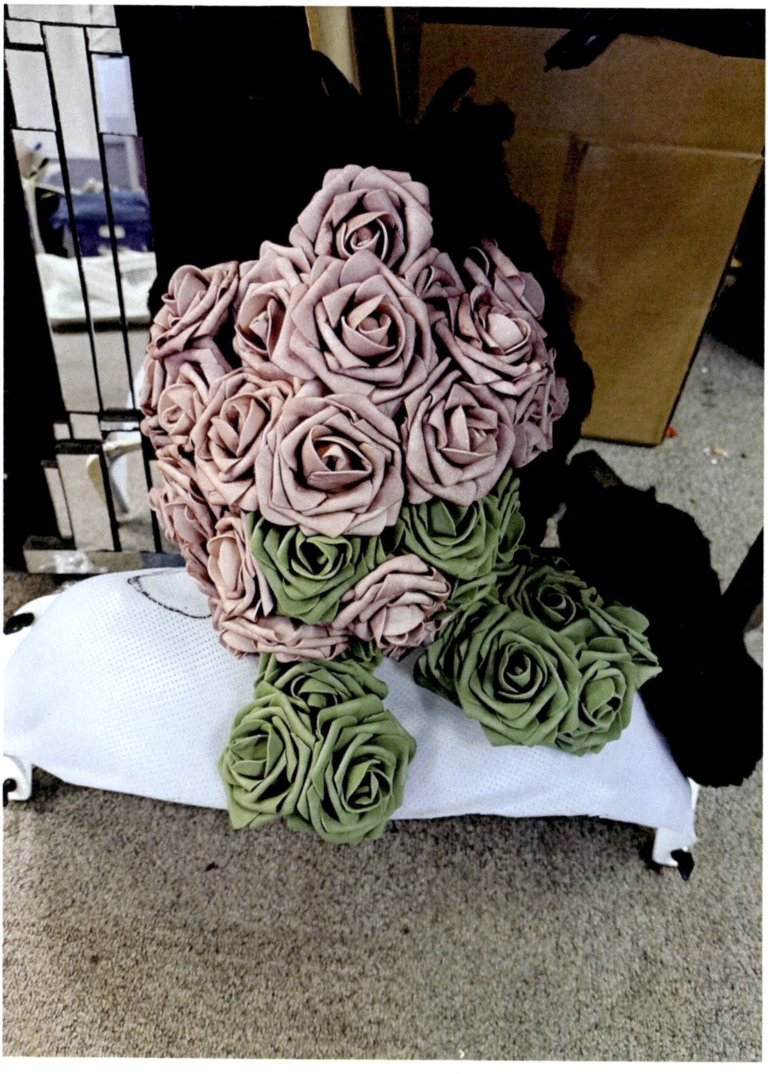

"REFLECTION" "FRIDA KAHLO INSPIRED MASK"

GREEN ROSES = CANCER IN BODY

GREEN SNAKE = SNEAKY SNAKE SPREADING CANCER.

Mask, Artwork and Picture by Melanie Griffiths.

PEOPLE DECORATE RADIOTHERAPY TREATMENT MASKS WITH FAVOURITE CHARACTERS SUCH AS WONDER WOMAN, CAPTAIN AMERICA, SPIDERMAN ETC. MEL HAS ALWAYS BEEN INSPIRED BY FRIDA'S STRENGTH, RESILIENCE & ART STYLE.

Special Thanks

To Guys Cancer Centre, Dr. Brady, Staff at the Radiotherapy Unit, Staff at Esther Ward, Nuclear Medicine Unit, Royal Free Hospital, Dr. Hassan, Dr. Holmes, Head and Neck Department, Lee High Road Dental Practice, Guys Dental Department, Celia – Macmillan Nurse, Art Network, Valerie Rosemary Griffiths R.I.P.

Thanks to everyone for their best wishes and prayers.
Xxx
Thank you to Debbie & Tog x

ALL PROCEEDS FROM THIS BOOK WILL GO TO MACMILLAN CANCER SUPPORT.